Strangers

By Dorothy Chlad

Illustrations by Lydia Halverson

CHILDRENS PRESS, CHICAGO

Library of Congress Cataloging in Publication Data

Chlad, Dorothy.
  Strangers.

  (Safety Town)
  Summary: Presents some rules for safe
behavior around people you don't know.
    1. Children and strangers—Juvenile
literature. [1. Strangers. 2. Safety.
3. Crime prevention] I. Halverson, Lydia, ill.
II. Title. III. Series: Chlad, Dorothy.
Safety Town.
HQ784.S8C48   362.8'8   81-18109
ISBN O-516-O1984-8   AACR2

Hi . . . my name is Susie.

I want to tell you
about strangers.

A stranger is someone you don't know.

Be careful when you go to school . . .

your friend's house . . .

the playground . . .

or the park.

Sometimes a
stranger might
want you to get
in a car or truck.

NEVER GET IN!

Never get in a
car or truck with a
stranger.

Try to remember what the stranger looked like. Remember what the car or truck looked like.

Tell your mother
or older brother. Tell
your father, sister,
or teacher.

To get close to
you a stranger
might give you
candy . . .

gum . . .

money . . .

toys . . .

or gifts.

Do not take
anything from a
stranger.

Sometimes
a stranger
might want to
talk to you.
Never talk
to a stranger.

If a stranger
touches you,
scream as loud
as you can.
Kick as hard
as you can.
And run away
as fast as
you can.

A stranger can be
short, tall, fat, or thin.

A stranger can be a
man or a woman.

A stranger can be
young or old . . . clean
or dirty.

There are strangers
in the city. There are
strangers in the country.

Stay with your
friends when you
go to school . . .

a friend's house . . .

the playground . . .

or an amusement
park.

It is safer to stay
with your friends.

When you go
shopping or to the
park, stay close to
your mom or dad
or older brother
and sister.

My friends and I
NEVER go with strangers!

Please remember
my safety rules.

Never talk to strangers.

Never get in a car or truck with a stranger.

Never go with a stranger.

About the Author

Dorothy Chlad, founder of the total concept of Safety Town, is recognized internationally as a leader in Preschool/Early Childhood Safety Education. She has authored six books on the program, and has conducted the only workshops dedicated to the concept. Under Mrs. Chlad's direction, the National Safety Town Center was founded; to promote the program through community involvement.

She has presented the importance of safety education at local, state, and national safety and education conferences, such as National Community Education Association, National Safety Council, and the American Driver and Traffic Safety Education Association. She serves as a member of several national committees, such as the Highway Traffic Safety Division and the Educational Resources Division of National Safety Council. Chlad was an active participant at the Sixth International Conference on Safety Education.

Dorothy Chlad continues to serve as a consultant for State Departments of Safety and Education. She has also consulted for the TV program "Sesame Street" and recently wrote this series of safety books for Childrens Press.

A participant of White House Conferences on safety, Dorothy Chlad has received numerous honors and awards including National Volunteer Activist and YMCA Career Woman of Achievement.

About the Artist

Lydia Halverson was born Lydia Geretti in midtown Manhattan. When she was two, her parents left New York and moved to Italy. Four years later her family returned to the United States and settled in the Chicago Area. Lydia attended the University of Illinois, graduating with a degree in fine arts. She worked as a graphic designer for many years before finally concentrating on book illustration.

Lydia lives with her husband and two cats in a suburb of Chicago and is active in several environmental organizations.